HOME GROWN

Study Guide

Essentials for Christian Parenting

Patricia Nederveld

ISBN 978-1-59255-492-8

10 9 8 7 6 5 4 3 2 1

CONTENTS

INTRODUCTION

This seven-session study is intended to be used with *Home Grown: Handbook for Christian Parenting* by Karen DeBoer. It offers your group of parents an opportunity to get together to share joys and challenges as you look for ways to nurture deeper, fuller faith in your children (and yourselves!).

We hope you'll find the handbook, along with this guide to discussing its key issues, a blessing and an encouragement to you as you follow Christ and invite your children to follow him too.

HOW TO USE THIS GUIDE

We suggest you set aside an hour for each of the seven sessions. You might also want to add an introductory session to get to know each other, learn a bit about everyone's family, and begin the habit of praying for each other. Also consider adding an extra session at the end to gather with your families for a meal, followed by a time of worship.

Each of the seven sessions in this guide corresponds to its chapter number in the handbook. You'll want to read the corresponding chapter *before* you gather so you can draw on its wisdom—and perhaps challenge some of its conclusions! Remember, no parenting guide is complete and infallible. The strength of this study will be your shared experiences and wisdom, complemented by the wise words of handbook author and mom of four, Karen DeBoer, and the experts whose advice she's incorporated into the questions and answers in the handbook.

HOW THE SESSIONS WORK

This guide encourages shared leadership; however, you may wish to appoint an informal leader to keep everyone on task and to pace the group as you work through the questions that capture your attention and address issues that are most important to you. Regardless of your leadership method, you'll want to roughly follow the session plan each week. Here's the sequence:

Think About It (10-15 minutes). Each session opens with a pointed question for parents. Check out how other parents have responded to the question (download video segments at www.HomeGrownParenting.org, or play them from the course DVD, sold separately). You'll also share your own responses to the same question during this opening step. Beginning with session 2, there will be time to look back over the previous week and talk about how you responded to the content of that session. And, in case the video option doesn't work for your group, there's an alternative suggestion for launching the session.

Talk About It (30-35 minutes). This section is the heart of the session. It consists of questions that follow up on the handbook chapter the group has read at home. We suggest you always begin with question 1, reading and discussing the Scripture together. After that, however, we encourage you to skim through the questions and choose the ones that are most important to your group. Aim to wrap up this part of the session about ten minutes before you plan to dismiss.

Pray About It. Notice that this step has no time frame—that's because the length of your prayer time may vary, and it shouldn't be rushed. As you get to know each other and the needs of each other's families, this will become a precious time. Don't hesitate to adjust the time given to discussion, leaving more time for prayer.

Live It (on your own time). Each week we'll give you a few ideas for following up on what you've learned by *doing* something. You can keep your experiences private, or you may want to build them into your group process, making commitments and deciding to be accountable to each other.

TIPS FOR LEARNING AND GROWING TOGETHER

Here are a few guidelines for making the most of this study and your group experience:

- **Come prepared each week**. Read the handbook chapter and note the focus statement for that week's discussion. Read the Scripture passages that undergird the material. Watch the accompanying video segment and glance over the questions in this study guide, noting those that seem the most compelling to you.
- **Come prepared to participate too**. You may feel that you come as a learner, but you also come as a parent with experience! Be willing to share what you're thinking and feeling with the others in your group.
- **Honor each other by listening**. Remember that families are different, parenting styles are different, and there's no such thing as a perfect parent! Speak your opinions honestly and be a good listener, encouraging others to do so as well, as together you search for ways to relate to your children that are effective and faithful to God's Word.
- **Honor time frames**. Try not to dominate the conversation; leave time for everyone to contribute their feelings and ideas. Begin and end on time to honor the busy schedules of each family in your group.

May God bless your time together as you seek to nurture your children in God's ways!

SESSION **1**

HOME IS WHERE THE HEART IS

SCRIPTURE

Deuteronomy 6; Luke 2:41-52

FOCUS

God calls parents to nurture the faith of their children.

**THINK ABOUT IT** (10-15 MINUTES)

What scares you most about being a Christian parent? That's the question parents in today's short video intro respond to—and it's a good one for us to think about as we begin this seven-week conversation.

If group members weren't able to watch the video prior to your meeting, watch it together now. Then take a few minutes to get to know each other by telling everyone a bit about who you are, who's in your family, and how you would answer this very personal question. (It's our hope that this study will help you support each other during the coming weeks—so get started today by sharing openly and offering encouragement to others from your own experience.)

We hope you've read chapter 1 of the handbook. It's all about God's call to Christian parents to nurture their kids' faith.

In case you've ever wondered about the relationship of your role as a parent and the role of the church in nurturing your child's faith, you'll be interested in a study done by the Search Institute to determine the influence of congregational life and religious education on the faith maturity of members (see p. 11 of the handbook).

The study discovered that the family's influence on the faith development of children and adolescents is greater than that of the religious education children and adolescents receive by being part of congregational life. That's statistical affirmation of God's call to us as Christian parents!

Twenty years have passed since this study was done by the Search Institute. What trends have you seen in our culture since 1990 that increase the urgency and importance of parents' role in nurturing the faith of their children?

For more research in this area, check out www.search-institute.org.

Of the two strongest connections to faith maturity, family religiousness is slightly more important than lifetime exposure to Christian education. The particular family experiences most tied to greater faith maturity are the frequency with which an adolescent talked with mother and father about faith, the frequency of family devotions, and the frequency with which parents and children together were involved in efforts, formal or informal, to help other people.

—Reprinted with permission from *Effective Christian Education: A national study of Protestant Congregations* - A summary report on faith, loyalty, and congregation life. © 1990 by Search Institute SM, Minneapolis, MN; www.search-institute.org. All rights reserved.

📖 TALK ABOUT IT (30-35 MINUTES)

Read Deuteronomy 6 together (we suggest you read it from *The Message*). Then discuss the following questions. If your time is limited, choose the questions that are most important to your group.

1. What do these words from God suggest about our role as godly parents? Where does the joy in Christian parenting come from?

2. How has the meaning of your baptism deepened for you over the years? How have you explained the meaning and significance of your child's baptism to him or her? Share some ways you help your family understand, remember, and celebrate their baptisms.

> In baptism God is making a public declaration that the child being baptized is loved by him, belongs to him, and is part of the community of faith. In essence, God is giving this child his/her primary identity.
>
> —Joyce Borger

3. How do you react to Proverbs 22:6 ("Train a child in the way he should go, and when he is old he will not turn from it" [NIV])? How do Bob De Moor's comments (see question 8 in the handbook) help you understand the verse as it relates to your role as a Christian parent?

4. Share something of your own faith development with the group. How does your own "faith biography" shape how you parent? If you came to faith later in life, what advantages might that have for how you nurture your child's faith? What challenges does it pose?

5. Think back over your own growing-up years and recall someone who intentionally "blessed" you. What did that blessing mean to you and to your emerging faith? How can we be more intentional about "blessing" our children?

6. In her book *Real Kids, Real Faith* (p. 10), Karen Marie Yust points out that faith is a gift from God, not a set of beliefs parents impart to their children. The spirituality of very young children, however, is shaped by perceptions, relationships, and experiences within their families. Suggest some ways that families can become more intentional about nurturing and shaping the faith of their little ones, beginning at birth.

Faith is a gift from God that lies dormant in children unless and until it is stirred up in them. It is like the yeast that bakers mix into bread: inactive until the baker adds a little warm water and begins kneading to spread the yeast throughout the dough. As parents, we can provide children with a rich spiritual environment that activates their faith and mixes it into their everyday lives.

—Karen-Marie Yust

7. Have you ever heard a parent say, "I'm not going to impose my faith on my kids. When they're old enough, they should be able to decide for themselves what they believe"? How would you respond to a friend who takes that point of view?

8. All families live by their own (often unwritten, even unacknowledged) mission statements. How would you summarize the "mission statement" of the family you grew up in? How would you edit or rewrite it to make it just right for your own family today?

9. In what ways do you hope this study and conversation with other parents will help you in your own faith—and in nurturing the faith of your children?

🔟 PRAY ABOUT IT

Set aside enough time to pray with and for each other at the end of each session. Be sure to pray in a general way for all of the parents and children represented in your group; but encourage everyone to share particular needs too. Keep everything said in your group confidential—only God needs to know each issue and challenge you're facing as you seek to become more godly in your parenting!

❗ LIVE IT

Here are a few suggestions for things you might do this week to follow up on the challenges and new insights you've received in your group session:

Talk about baptism

Do a little family research and set aside some time (at a meal, at bedtime) to tell your children the story of their baptisms if they've been baptized. Mark the dates on a family calendar and covenant together to celebrate each baptism on its anniversary date in the year ahead. Talk about what it means to be a child of God and a part of God's family.

Create a family mission statement

If you have older children who will understand the purpose and meaning of a family mission statement, take a half-hour after dinner or before bedtime to develop a simple statement that reflects your family's faith and purpose in God's world.

Find a family life verse

Invite your children to share favorite verses from Scripture that might serve as a family (or individual) guiding verse. Write out the verse(s) you decide on together and tuck them in your family Bible or post them on the refrigerator.

SESSION **2**

FEARFULLY AND WONDERFULLY MADE

 **SCRIPTURE**

Psalm 139; Matthew 21:14-17

 FOCUS

Parents can rely on God's loving guidance as they seek to nurture their children's faith.

THINK ABOUT IT (10-15 MINUTES)

What has been your greatest joy in watching your children's faith grow? That's the question posed by today's short video. If group members weren't able to watch the video prior to your meeting, watch it together as a way of beginning your conversation. Then take a few minutes to share your own feelings and experiences in response to the question the parents answer in the video.

You might also want to set aside a few minutes to invite each other to share ways you've followed up on the discussion from last time. Has anyone talked with their children about baptism, developed a family mission statement, or chosen a life verse for their family?

Another possibility for beginning today's conversation about God's guidance for parents is to read and discuss the short case study that follows.

KEVIN AND MARIA

Kevin and Maria are in their early thirties and have just celebrated their fifth wedding anniversary. They're also looking forward to celebrating the arrival of their first baby, a girl, just three months away. The nursery is ready, complete with baby Jessica's name painted on the door.

They're excited, happy—and more than a little apprehensive. In fact, fears and misgivings have been nagging at them lately. Not that they've talked about it together—they've just experienced it in the quiet of their own hearts, on the way to work, working out at the gym, lying awake in bed at night.

"This is something we've planned for, something we really, really want! Why do I feel this way?" wonders Maria.

"Maria seems so sure—but I'm scared! Scared for me, scared for us, scared for this new baby!" thinks Kevin.

Kevin and Maria have plenty of questions, and not many answers. Do we have what it takes to be good parents? Should one of us stop working? Which one? If we do, how will we ever afford to move out of this tiny apartment? Why would we want to bring a child into a world full of war, environmental destruction, famine, and discrimination? How will we ever help her grow as a child of God, resisting things in our culture that we can hardly resist ourselves?

How would you counsel Kevin and Maria? What encouragement would you have for them? What advice would you give them?

TALK ABOUT IT (30-35 MINUTES)

Spend time reading Psalm 139 and discussing the following questions together. If your time is limited, choose the questions that are most important to your group.

1. How might you use this psalm in a conversation with a young couple like Kevin and Maria? What does this psalm say to you—as a child of God, as a parent?

2. In the book *Perspectives on Children's Spiritual Formation*, Scottie May says that children are born as spiritual beings. How does this fit with the words of Psalm 139? What does May's statement suggest about God's work, the church's efforts, and parents' influence on the faith development of their children?

> The Christian spirituality of children is nurtured through openness to the Holy Spirit as mediated by life within the faith community. It is strengthened by corporate uses of Scripture, forms of prayer, hymns, ritual and sacraments, retreats, and the cycles of the liturgical year, which include feasts and celebrations. This nurture cannot happen in isolation.
>
> If the context for the child is not Christian, the child still has the quality of spirituality with accompanying questions about life, self, and meaning. The environment then strongly influences the direction that spirituality takes— whether a child finds her or his life in Jesus Christ or not.
>
> —Scottie May et al. in *Children Matter*, Eerdmans 2005, p. 50

3. Check out the list of spiritual characteristics of children on pages 42-48 of the handbook. Share with the group the ages of your children and how the characteristics fit them (or don't fit them). Trade stories that highlight the growing faith you see in your kids—and praise God for it!

4. Note the references to prayer in the spiritual characteristics list on pages 42-48 of the handbook. Spend a few minutes talking about the ways your children express themselves in prayer. It's easy to offer prayers on behalf of our children or to teach them memorized prayers rather than inviting them to use their own thoughts and words to talk to God. Suggest some ways we can help children develop their own prayer language and habits from a young age.

Dear God,
Instead of letting people die and having to make new ones, why don't you just keep the ones you have now?
—Jane

Dear God,
I bet it is very hard for You to love all of everybody in the whole world. There are only four people in our family and I can never do it.
—Nan

—posted on www.ksu.edu/wwparent/humor/god.htm

5. Parents mess up! And we certainly don't have all the answers! Handbook author Karen DeBoer suggests that we should let our children in on the reality of our own frailty as Christ's followers—and as Christian parents. How easy is that for you? Could doing that weaken your influence over your kids? Suggest some ways to be more intentional about using our own weakness to teach our children about God's grace.

6. What happens when you experience doubts or question God's ways? Do a believer's doubts diminish his or her faith? Will your children's faith be diminished as a result of your own doubts? And how exactly do we deal with the faith questions our children ask us when we aren't even sure of the answers ourselves? Spend some time talking about these challenging questions.

7. Parenting gets more complicated when the second (third, fourth) child joins the family group. Different personalities beg for different approaches to boundary setting, discipline techniques, and so forth.

   What common principles do you apply across the board in your parenting? How have you had to adapt or tailor some of your approaches to your kids' personalities and responses?

8. In the 1970s, advice columnist Ann Landers posed this question to her readers: If you had to do it all over again, would you have children? Of the mind-blowing 10,000 responses she received, 70 percent said no! Do you think the result would have been different if she had asked that question only of Christian parents? Why or why not?

9. What is your prayer for your children? Take a few minutes to write a short prayer here. Share it with the group if you wish.

⟨⟩ PRAY ABOUT IT

Take time to pray with and for each other at the end of this session. Be sure to pray in a general way for all the parents and children represented in your group, but encourage everyone to share particular needs too. (If you took time to write individual prayers for your children, you might want to incorporate those into your prayer time.)

⚠ LIVE IT

Here are a few suggestions for things you might do this week to follow up on the challenges and new insights you've received from each other:

Check your MQ (model quotient)

Your kids watch, listen, and learn from your life and the way you live out your faith. Take a five- to ten-minute break with a cup of coffee or tea this week and devote that time to reflecting on how it's going. Ask yourself
- how your words reflect your faith to your family.
- how your actions reflect your faith to your family.
- how your "mess ups" (and theirs!) and the way you deal with them teach your family about God's grace.
- how your doubts, expressed honestly, provide teachable moments for helping your kids ask faith questions.

Write letters to your children

Write a short note to each of your children, reminding them that God knew them before they even came into your family. Tell them how much God loves them—and how much you do too.

Pray together

Try out a new way of praying together as a family. For example, rather than saying a mealtime prayer yourself, invite *everyone* to contribute—especially your littlest family members. Begin simply, asking each one to add to your prayer by thanking God for one thing they felt grateful for today.

SETTING BOUNDARIES, SHOWING GRACE

 **SCRIPTURE**

Ephesians 6:1-4; Colossians
3:20-21; Genesis 1, 2

FOCUS

Parents and children need to follow
God's example of setting boundaries
and extending grace to each other.

THINK ABOUT IT (10-15 MINUTES)

Share an experience of setting boundaries for and extending grace to your children—that's the request to parents in today's video segment. If group members weren't able to watch the video prior to your meeting, watch it together as a way of beginning your conversation about setting boundaries and extending grace to your kids.

Take a few minutes to share your own feelings and experiences in response to this conversation starter too.

You might also want to set aside a few minutes to invite each other to share ways you've followed up on the discussion from last time. Have any of the parents in the group written letters to their children or tried praying in a new way as a family?

Another possibility for introducing today's discussion: talk about parenting styles and their influence on kids' behavior and development. This has been a key area of research over the past several decades. Two particularly interesting and helpful studies ("Socialization in the Context of the Family: Parent-Child Interaction" by Maccoby & Martin, 1983 and "The Influence of Parenting Style on Adolescent Competence and Substance Use" by Diana Baumrind, 1991) identify four styles of parenting, particularly around issues of boundaries and control. They also assess the consequences of each parenting style for kids as they grow into adulthood.

Here are four parenting styles as defined by these two studies:

- **Indulgent**—indulgent parents tend to be permissive, responsive, lenient, non-directive, and not very demanding of their kids when it comes to standards of behavior.
- **Authoritarian**—authoritarian parents tend to be *very* demanding but not very responsive to their kids; they're highly directive, structured, and obedience-oriented.
- **Authoritative**—these parents tend to be *both* demanding (set clear standards for behavior) and responsive (supportive in helping their children learn to take responsibility for their actions).
- **Uninvolved**—these parents are neither demanding nor responsive. They may even be neglectful of their kids' needs.

What do you think the consequences of each style might be for kids' behavior? What might be the consequences for their development in areas of social competence and taking responsibility for their actions?

Spend a few minutes sharing your perceptions of your own parenting styles.

Assign one member of the group to check out the studies online this week and report back next time. Here's a helpful website: www.athealth.com (search for "parenting styles").

Parenting style captures two important elements of parenting: parental responsiveness and parental demandingness (Maccoby & Martin, 1983). Parental responsiveness (also referred to as parental warmth or supportiveness) refers to "the extent to which parents intentionally foster individuality, self-regulation, and self-assertion by being attuned, supportive, and acquiescent to children's special needs and demands" (Baumrind, 1991, p. 62). Parental demandingness (also referred to as behavioral control) refers to "the claims parents make on children to become integrated into the family whole, by their maturity demands, supervision, disciplinary efforts and willingness to confront the child who disobeys" (Baumrind, 1991, pp. 61-62).

📖 TALK ABOUT IT (30-35 MINUTES)

Spend time reading Ephesians 6:1-4 together. Then discuss the following questions. If your time is limited, choose the questions that are most important to your group.

1. How does this work at your house? What does it mean not to "exasperate your children" or "crush their spirits"? How does your understanding of these passages shape your parenting style?

2. How do you interpret the common proverb "Spare the rod and spoil the child," which is based on Proverbs 13:24? How does it help you (or not help you) in your efforts to set boundaries for your children? Note: Parents have widely differing views on spanking, so if you decide to discuss this topic, you may need to schedule an extra session! Be sure to extend grace to those with whom you disagree.

3. In a two-parent family, why is it so important that both parents practice a similar and consistent approach to setting boundaries for their children? What are the particular challenges for those of you who are divorced parents, single parents, step-parents, or parents in blended families?

4. The handbook suggests that there are many different "right" ways to raise children. Have you found resources (other people, books, magazines) that are helping you find *your* way? Share them with the group and tell how they've helped you set a course for your family.

5. Locate a copy of the baptism vows formulated by your denomination and read the form together. What promises did you make when you brought a child to be baptized? How do the promises you made relate to the way you set boundaries for your kids, discipline them when necessary, and extend the grace of Christ to them?

6. Spend some time talking about handbook questions 40 and 41 (Is it OK to be angry with my child? How do I deal with my anger?). The handbook suggests that it's OK to feel anger, but what's more important is how you handle it. Do you think that's true? Why or why not? What's your greatest challenge in communicating your anger to your child—and what suggestion(s) for dealing with anger did you find helpful?

7. Parents are the primary shapers of their children's values and beliefs, but friends play a big part too. How do you help your kids choose their friends? How do you deal with it when their friends' values and beliefs are quite different from yours? What did you find helpful in the handbook discussion of this challenge to parents (see questions 50 and 51)?

8. In his book *Forgive and Forget*, Lewis B. Smedes says this:

> Forgiving is love's toughest work, and love's biggest risk. If you twist it into something it was never meant to be, it can make you a doormat or an insufferable manipulator. Forgiving seems almost unnatural. Our sense of fairness tells us people should pay for the wrong they do. But forgiving is love's power to break nature's rule (p. 12).

Why is forgiving so tough? Does forgiving your children ever leave you feeling like a doormat—or a manipulator? Share some family forgiveness stories and what you've learned (and what your children have learned) from them.

Suggest some good ways to teach children about the meaning and power of forgiveness.

9. How do we keep our kids safe, especially from abuse by others? That, too, is a burning question for parents today. Share some ways in which you help your children remain outgoing and open to healthy friendships and relationships while at the same time remaining alert to people who might misuse their friendship or abuse them in some way. Is there something more (or different?) you can do based on your reading of the material in the handbook? What can you do to make sure your church and its kids' programs are as safe as possible?

> When someone you know has hurt your child, your pain as a parent and protector is so great that it is almost impossible for you to react. This means you must seek outside help.
>
> —Beth Swagman

☉ PRAY ABOUT IT

Take time to pray with and for each other at the end of this session. Be sure to pray in a general way for all the parents and children represented in your group; but encourage everyone to share their needs, particularly in the area of setting boundaries and extending grace within the family.

⚠ LIVE IT

Here are a few suggestions for things you might do this week to follow up on the challenges and new insights you've received from each other:

Analyze your parenting style

If the brief conversation about parenting styles at the beginning of today's session intrigued you, check out www.athealth.com (search for "parenting styles"). Do the results of the research surprise you?

What's your parenting style? What changes would you like God to help you make in the area of setting boundaries and extending grace to your children? (If there's someone in the study group you feel close to, ask him or her to pray for your efforts to fine-tune or adjust your parenting style.)

Keep a boundaries/grace journal for the week

To stay tuned in to the issue of boundaries and grace, keep a log this week of boundary issues that surface in your family. Jot down how you handled them, how your children responded, and how "gracefully" you handled each situation and its outcome.

Check out your church's safety policy

Call or e-mail the person at your church who's in charge of ministry to children and youth; ask whether the church has a formal safety policy that guards kids against abuse by staff or volunteers in the church programs. If there is no safety policy, consider volunteering your services (or the group's) in researching and proposing a plan for putting such guidelines in place.

SESSION **4**

DAILY DETAILS, SPECIAL CELEBRATIONS

 **SCRIPTURE**

Joshua 4:21-24; Psalm 78:1-7

 FOCUS

Parents nurture their children's faith through everyday rituals and activities as well as through special milestones and celebrations.

THINK ABOUT IT (10-15 MINUTES)

What's your most meaningful family faith practice? That's the kickoff question today's video segment poses. If group members weren't able to watch the video prior to your meeting, watch it together as a way of beginning your discussion. Take a few minutes to share with the group a faith practice that's been meaningful to your family over the years—or share a practice you're just beginning.

You might also want to set aside a few minutes to share ways you've followed up on the discussion from last time. Has anyone done some additional research on parenting styles? (Did you learn that the *authoritative parent*, who sets limits while giving explanations, is generally the most effective in shaping positive behavior in kids?) Or perhaps someone in the group has benefited from new insights through keeping a boundaries/grace journal since you last met. Take time to share your thoughts and support each other.

Another possibility for introducing today's discussion: react to the David Anderson quote (see box). In his book, a worthwhile read for church leaders and parents alike, Anderson insists that the home is the primary incubator for nurturing vibrant faith in children. He contends that the church has to be far more than "family-friendly"—it must encourage, support, enable, and help equip families, acknowledging that the home is an expression of the church in which the Spirit uses caring relationships to form and grow faith.

> To a significant degree, what has been lost in the church is the value of family itself. The Christian community has not sufficiently defined or promoted a viable life of faith for home and family. With all the cultural, political, and religious talk about 'family values,' this observation might seem a bit odd. However, there is a big difference between the rhetoric of family values and the actual practice of valuing families as a God-given source of faith formation.
>
> As some talk of family values, others react negatively to it as a politicized concept. The negative reaction tends to undervalue the gift of daily life relationships in and through the home. Between these two cultural poles is a third way, a way that does not limit the life of the family to political sound bites and does not throw out the value of family life with the bath water of family values. The third way is to recapture the role of the home in passing on faith, values, and character formation.
>
> —David Anderson, *From the Great Omission to Vibrant Faith: The Role of the Home in Renewing the Church*, Vibrant Faith Ministries 2009, p. 25

Do you agree with Anderson? How would you define the role of the home and the role of the church in nurturing children's faith? What can parents do to strengthen the partnership? How does your congregation fulfill the vows they made at the time of your child(ren)'s baptism?

📋 TALK ABOUT IT (30-35 MINUTES)

Spend time reading Psalm 78:1-7 together (we suggest you use *The Message* for this one). Then discuss the following questions. If your time is limited, choose the questions that are the most important to your group.

1. Which words or phrases from Psalm 78 jump out at you and challenge you? Which give you encouragement and hope as you raise your own kids in the faith?

2. Read the story of Joshua and the stones from Joshua 4:21-24. How does the pile of stones function for God's people? (Can you think of other places in Scripture where stones serve a similar purpose?) Share some examples from your own family life in which you've created—or could create—visible reminders of God's love and faithfulness.

3. Spend a few minutes talking about family prayer: When and where do you pray together? Who prays? What form do your family prayers usually take? Check out the suggestions in the answer to question 67 of the handbook for ways to pray at home. Share with the group some that you've tried. Commit to trying a new way of praying with your family in the week ahead. (And don't forget the last suggestion: silence before God is a wonderful practice to teach your children, even at an early age!)

4. Teachable moments are everywhere! Your children's ordinary everyday experiences offer you wonderful opportunities for faith conversations and faith nurture. Think back over the past week at your house for examples of teachable moments you grabbed and used . . . as well as some you wish you could recapture! In the midst of our hectic lives, what could we do to become better listeners and observers, attuning ourselves to teachable moments in our life with kids?

5. Christmas and other holidays might be described as "extended teachable moments." Share with the group some of the things you do to keep your children focused on God at Christmas, at Easter, and other holidays. What traditions from your childhood have you continued in your own family's observance of special days and seasons?

6. Describe for the group your own faith journey, with a focus on the milestones along the way. Then shift your conversation to your children and the faith milestones you've observed in their young lives, beginning with baptism. Are children considered full members of the body of Christ in your church? Which faith milestones, if any, does your congregation celebrate? How might the milestone concept be expanded so that families and

congregations become more intentional about recognizing and celebrating faith milestones of children and adults?

We don't usually need to convince our children that they are members of our family—they just are. We include them from the moment they are born or adopted. While we treat our children differently when they grow up or as they reach adulthood, we don't make them wait until then to become full members of the family. As a church, however, it seems that we sometimes don't really consider children full members of the body. We see them as *potential* members, people who will be members when they get older.

—Robert J. Keeley, *Helping Our Children Grow in Faith*, Baker 2008, p. 29. Used by permission.

7. Take a poll around the circle—how many people wish their family lives were less hectic? Most of today's families have a hard time finding "together" time for praying, listening to Scripture and to each other, and learning and growing in the faith. How does your family approach this challenge? What works for you? Share your thoughts with the group. Encourage and challenge each other to make time for God in your family life.

8. Does the quote from *Embracing Parents* (see box) connect with your experience as you seek to nurture your kids' faith? Where do you draw support for this challenge? What additional support or "connectedness" would be helpful to you?

Research shows that parents are more effective when they have the support and encouragement of those around them. Whether the support comes from a spouse, another adult family member, extended family, friends, or people within the community—or best of all, all of these places—that support makes a big difference.

Despite public perception that parents should be solely responsible for raising kids and are doing a poor job of parenting, research clearly shows that those who have strong, supportive connections are more likely to parent better and have better relationships with their children.

— Jolene and Eugene Roehlkepartain, *Embracing Parents: How Your Congregation Can Strengthen Families*, Abingdon Press 2004, p. 15. Used by permission.

9. Celebrating "Sabbath" is far more than making a list of what to do and not do on Sunday! As handbook author Karen DeBoer suggests, it's a God-given pause, an antidote to the hassle of our hectic daily lives. How do you celebrate Sabbath? How does your family celebrate Sabbath? Read aloud through the list of suggestions in the answer to question 77 of the handbook and find at least one that you'd like to try with your family in the week ahead. Share it with the group; commit to reporting back to each other next time.

⊕ PRAY ABOUT IT

Take time to pray with and for each other at the end of this session. Pray in a general way for all the parents and children represented in your group, and encourage everyone to share needs for the coming week and your efforts to keep Christ at the center of each day in your family's life. To end your prayer and this session on a joyful note, ask someone to read the words of Psalm 100 for the group.

⚠ LIVE IT

Here are a few suggestions for things you might do this week to follow up on the challenges and new insights you've received from each other:

Find support

Where do you find personal support and encouragement for your parenting? Be intentional about asking someone to pray for you and your particular needs in the coming days and weeks. It might be a fellow small group member, a like-minded friend or colleague, or an older person in your congregation who's raised children in the faith and knows your challenges as well as your hopes for your children. When you find someone who is committed to praying for you, make sure you have regular conversations about your ongoing needs and how God has answered your encourager's prayers for you.

Get ready for Christmas

Give some thought to adding an Advent ritual to your family treasury of customs and practices. Gather materials for making a Jesse tree, an Advent calendar, or an Advent wreath. Read up on the tradition, its origins, its meaning for people of faith. Involve your kids in preparing and using this new means of staying focused on Christ during Advent and the celebration of Christmas.

Find family time

Schedule a family meeting to talk with your kids about your busy lifestyle. Together make a list of everything your family does in a normal week. What activities on your list are most important to you (write a "1" next to them). Do the same with second- and third-level priorities. Is there anything you can do less of in order to have more time to talk together—and to talk to God together?

SESSION **5**

CHALLENGES AND TRANSITIONS

 **SCRIPTURE**

Genesis 28 and portions of 48-50;
2 Corinthians 1:3-7 or John 11:17-27

 FOCUS

Parents can deal honestly with difficult challenges and issues that come with raising children in today's culture because we can be sure God is with us in our struggles.

THINK ABOUT IT (10-15 MINUTES)

What's the most challenging question one of your kids has ever asked you?
That's the video lead-in question for today's session. If group members weren't able to watch the video prior to your meeting, you might want to watch it together as a way of beginning your discussion. Take a few minutes to share with the group some of the tough questions your children have asked you over the years. If you had good answers for them, share those too!

You might also want to set aside a few minutes to talk about how you followed up on the discussion from last time. Has anyone found a confidant who's committed to lifting you up in prayer as you seek to nurture your children's love for the Lord? Or did you find time to analyze your busy family schedule together? Have you tried to make some changes? Take a few minutes to encourage and support each other in your efforts.

Here's another possibility for introducing today's discussion about difficult situations in our lives as families: read the case study (see box below) and talk about it together. Here are some questions you might ponder:

- Put yourselves into the minds and hearts of Ben and Trish—what do you think they're thinking and feeling?
- Put yourselves into the minds and hearts of Jesse and Erika—what might they be thinking and feeling?
- From your own experience with divorce (your own, a friend's, a family member's), what might you do or say to help Ben, Trish, and their children?
- How does your faith influence how you relate to family and friends in divorce situations?

BEN AND TRISH

Ben and Trish have been married for twelve years. They have two children, Jesse (age 9) and Erika (age 5), whom they dearly love. But they don't love each other—they've decided to divorce. Preliminaries went fairly well—finding attorneys, filing the papers, talking about who gets what (including the kids), and deciding to keep things "friendly" for Jesse and Erika's sake. They've even told the kids what's about to happen—though telling them exactly *why* was more than a small challenge! As it turns out, breaking the news to Jesse and Erika was the beginning of one challenge after another for everyone.

Jesse received the news quietly, asking few questions, shedding few tears. But since that first conversation he's seemed depressed and often says his stomach hurts. His teacher has called to express concern (and surprise) over his failing academic work, his negative attitude in the classroom, and his aggressive behavior on the playground. She wonders if everything is OK at home.

Erika, always more outgoing and expressive, tells her mommy and daddy that they may *not* get divorced. She wonders out loud if they'll stay together if she's a better girl . . . maybe it's her fault that they're not happy together. She's also reverted back to behaviors like using baby talk, rebelling at bath time, and deliberately misbehaving in public situations. Occasionally she also wets her bed during the night.

Ben and Trish are unprepared for what's happening! In the midst of their own turmoil over the coming divorce, they need more than ever to attend to the emotional needs of their children. But they're not "together" about how to face these unexpected challenges.

🗨 TALK ABOUT IT (30-35 MINUTES)

Spend time reading Scripture and discussing these questions together. If your time is limited, choose the questions that are most important to your group.

1. Read 2 Corinthians 1:3-7 together. What words and phrases offer you hope for the challenges you face in your family life? What words or phrases suggest a role Christians should play in the lives of others who are in the midst of challenges, changes, and suffering?

2. Do your kids worry? Are you in touch with the things in their lives that trouble them? How can you help your children learn to trust Jesus in times of change and challenge while not communicating to them a false promise that Jesus will immediately make everything OK?

3. Helping children understand when family members suffer from depression or other mental illness requires sensitivity and honesty. Share some of your experiences, either positive or negative, in learning about and dealing with the mental illness of a loved one or a friend. (Take time to pray for group members for whom this is a current challenge.)

4. The death of a family member or friend provides an unexpected teachable moment for parents and children. Share an experience you've had in helping a child (yours or someone else's) begin to understand death—and to grieve in a healthy way. How would you respond to questions about the relationship between God's love and the pain that death causes us?

5. Talk a bit more about divorce and its effects on kids. What *spiritual* effects might divorce have on children? How might divorce affect family faith practices? How might it influence children's understanding of God's love? If some members of your group are newly divorced, encourage them in this difficult transition. What are their particular challenges? Re-entering the dating scene, managing financially, sharing custody of their children in a healthy and positive way? Take time to pray personally for each person currently in a divorce transition.

6. "But we like it here—we don't want to move!" How should a parent respond? How might a parent help his or her kids understand the reason for and deal with the trauma of moving to a new home, a new school, perhaps a new city that's far away from everything that's loved and familiar? What difference does your family's faith make in stressful transitions like moving? How have you tried to anchor your children's trust in God's love so they'll have a firm foundation when life is difficult?

7. Read the quote below by author Robert J. Keeley (see box). We *do* want our children to sense our deep faith and our willingness to entertain faith questions that rise out of troubled circumstances. But what happens when one parent's faith perspective is different from the other parent's? Or when one parent is not a believer? Which do you think speaks louder to your children, your words or the faith you model? Why? How do you respond to contributor Judy Cook's suggestion (see handbook question 81) that sometimes we need to simply give a difficult situation over to God and wait for the leading of the Holy Spirit?

> Children who live in difficult circumstances can have deep questions about their faith. Children who have been abused, for example, or children whose parents have divorced can ask very difficult questions, and we want to be able to give them good answers. We want these children to know that we have a solid faith, a faith that is dependable when things are not easy, because our God is dependable. We also want them to know that we have a faith that is rich enough and deep enough to entertain difficult questions.
>
> —Robert Keeley, *Helping Our Children Grow in Faith*, Baker 2008, p. 13

8. Check out handbook question 83 for a discussion of adoption. Contributor Ron Nydam suggests that adoptive families are formed out of a child's loss, which suggests that adoptive parents play a formative role in helping their children develop healthy identities and experience deep love and belonging. This takes wisdom and work! If there are members of your group who have children by adoption, listen to their stories, offer them encouragement, and spend a few minutes in prayer for their particular family needs.

9. Talk about other changes and challenges your families are facing (or have faced). Share ways you have helped your kids understand change in their lives, accept it, and grow from it, knowing that God is faithful.

⟨⟩ PRAY ABOUT IT

Take time to pray with and for each other at the end of this session. Pray in a general way for all the parents and children represented in your group, but focus especially on the current family challenges and crises that group members have shared. As always, respect each other and keep your conversations and prayer requests confidential.

! LIVE IT

Here are a few suggestions for things you might do this week to follow up on the challenges and new insights you've received from each other:

Remember a loved one

Take a few minutes with your child (or children) to look through a family scrapbook and reminisce about a loved family member who has died. Have fun talking about that person and his or her place in your lives. Then use the opportunity to talk honestly about that loved one's death, how sad it felt, and how you've experienced God's healing and comfort in the days (months, years) since you were separated from that person by death.

Pray for friends

Perhaps your family life is relatively trouble-free and uncomplicated at the moment. Praise God for that together! And pray for friends or relatives who may be facing a new challenge or experiencing a crisis—divorce, death of a dear one, serious illness. Your children will catch the concern and compassion you show, while learning at an early age the power of prayer. Be sure to remind them of God's faithful presence in your own family's life as well as in the lives of those you pray for.

Talk about it

On the other hand, perhaps you're feeling burdened by a current challenge or change in your own family's situation. Chances are, if you're heavy-hearted, your kids have noticed and have questions of their own. Take time with them, one by one, to talk about it privately, to entertain their questions (even the hard ones!), and to pray with them.

SESSION **6**

TIME, TALENTS, AND TITHES

 **SCRIPTURE**

Genesis 12:1-3; Luke 10:25-37

 FOCUS

Parents help shape their children's faith by engaging as a family in God's mission in the world.

🔍 THINK ABOUT IT (10-15 MINUTES)

Share something you've done with your kids to serve God by serving others.
That's the video lead-in for today's session. If group members weren't able to watch the video prior to your meeting, watch it together as a way of beginning your discussion. Take a few minutes to share with the group some of the ways in which the families in your group have used their particular gifts of time, talent, and tithes to reach out to others in the name of Jesus.

You might also want to set aside a few minutes to talk about how you followed up on the discussion from last time. Did you find an opportunity to talk with your children about a change that's currently affecting your family? Or perhaps you found a moment to remember a loved one who died recently, giving thanks for that person's life and comforting each other as you grieve his or her absence. Did you find an opportunity to remind your children of God's loving presence in your family's life as you face particular challenges or struggle with changes? Take a few minutes to encourage and support each other in your efforts to help your children trust God's leading.

Here's another possibility for introducing today's discussion that focuses on helping our children sense the importance of engaging in God's mission in the world. Read the quote below from the foreword of the book *A Kid's Guide to Giving*, written by fourteen-year-old Freddi Zeiler. Use the follow-up questions to start your thinking and conversation about helping our kids see themselves as God's people engaging in God's mission in this world.

I always thought my life was normal. I lived in a house with my mom, dad, and two younger sisters. My mom drove me to school every morning in our van. I would learn about fractions or mammals or Benjamin Franklin and then come home and do my homework and have dinner with my family. That didn't seem unusual to me. I did it every day—so did everyone else I knew, and so that was it. Nothing special. And that's what I thought for the first thirteen years of my life.

Then in seventh grade, I started watching the news and reading newspapers. I started to learn about things that were going on in other parts of the world. I learned that there were kids in the world whose families couldn't afford to send them to school; instead, these kids had to work to earn money so their families could buy food. I learned about people who didn't have money for medicine when they were sick, and I learned that the environment was being damaged by pollution. I learned that trees were being cut down from rain forests, and animals were losing their homes.

All of these things made me realize that my life wasn't normal. . . .

—Freddi Zeiler, *A Kid's Guide to Giving*, Innovative Kids 2006, p. 7

- How would you compare Freddi's "awakening" to the needs of the world to your own experience growing up? To your children's experience?
- Freddi's perspective on giving of oneself comes from a humanitarian desire to help others in need, to make a difference in a world beset by problems. What is your/your family's motivation for investing your time, talents, and tithes in caring for one another and for our world? What role does your faith play in your attitudes and actions?

💬 TALK ABOUT IT (30-35 MINUTES)

Spend time reading Scripture and discussing the following questions together. If your time is limited, choose the questions that are most important to your group.

1. Read Luke 10:25-37 together and talk about the ironies in Jesus' parable. Do you see any of these same inconsistencies today? How does your congregation live out Jesus' parting words to the young lawyer: "Go and do likewise"? What kinds of models do your children have for obeying Jesus' command? Share some positive examples.

2. In question 89 of the handbook, author Karen DeBoer confesses her aversion to the little green compost pail under her sink. What reservations and resistances keep us from becoming more fully engaged in God's mission in this world? What can we learn from our kids that might help us resolve to pursue a more stewardly and compassionate lifestyle?

3. How early can we begin to teach children to recognize the needs of others and to give of themselves? Freddi Zeiler (see box on p. 44) says she was thirteen before she sensed that the world was far more troubled than her own life was. Can we speed up that awareness in our own kids? How?

4. It's hard, living in our individualistic culture, for us to resist the notion that what we possess is ours and ours alone—we've earned it, after all! How can we as Christians counteract such thinking? How can we help our kids understand what it means to live gratefully as stewards of the gifts we receive from God?

5. Teaching very young children to share toys with their siblings and playmates seems like a logical place to start, but is it possible? That's a question every frustrated parent of a toddler asks! Check out the handbook answer to question 90 and talk about the suggestions offered by the author. What has worked for you?

6. The title of this session suggests three ways individuals and families can invest themselves and become participants in God's mission in this world: by sharing their time, talents, and tithes. Spend a few minutes talking about each of these three and ways your family has found to share. Is there a particular area that seems especially challenging for you? Encourage each other to engage your families in conversation about each area, with an eye toward refreshing your family commitments to serving God by serving others.

7. American humorist Arnold Glasow once said, "Parents can tell, but never teach, unless they practice what they preach." How does his wit and wisdom apply to God's call to us and our families to use the gifts he's given us to serve others? How much should we tell our children about how we use our time, our talents, and our money for causes outside ourselves? Apart from our telling them, what do our children learn from observing our attitudes and actions? How can we become more intentional about "practicing what we preach"?

8. Check out the list of family-friendly stewardship ideas handbook author Karen DeBoer lists in question 95. Which ideas have you and your family implemented in your day-to-day lives? What are the challenges you've faced in changing your attitudes and behavior in order to become more stewardly? Add to the list by sharing ideas that your own kids have suggested or other strategies your family has implemented.

9. Check out the list of family service projects in handbook question 100. If you've tried any of them (or done something that's not listed) share your experience and your learnings with the group. What challenges did you encounter? What was the most important benefit of the experience for your children? For you? For your faith?

✪ PRAY ABOUT IT

Read aloud the quote in the box on page 49 from *Our World Belongs to God*; then take time to pray with and for each other, asking God to attune you and your families to his mission in this world. Give God thanks for the gifts of time, talents, and money, and ask his help as you seek to involve your children in using your family's gifts to help redeem God's world.

The Spirit calls all members
to embrace God's mission
in their neighborhoods
and in the world:
to feed the hungry,
bring water to the thirsty,
welcome the stranger,
clothe the naked,
care for the sick,
and free the prisoner.
We repent of leaving this work to a few,
for this mission is central to our being.

—*Our World Belongs to God: A Contemporary Testimony.*
Faith Alive Christian Resources 2008, p. 24.

LIVE IT

Here are a few suggestions for things you might do this week to follow up on the challenges and new insights you've received from each other:

Plan a project with your preschooler

Little ones aren't too young to understand what it means to serve others—or to do it! Plan a way to visit someone who needs cheering up (young children bring smiles and joy to people who are elderly, ill, or discouraged). Bake cookies with your child; then deliver them together and stay for a visit. Use the outing as a teachable moment, reminding your little one that a very good way to show we love Jesus is to show we love and care for others.

Plan a group service project

Consider choosing a service project that the families represented by your group members can engage in together (revisit the list in question 100 of the handbook to start your thinking). Ask one or two members of your group to coordinate schedules and logistics. After completing your project, get together for a snack or a meal to talk about your experience.

Talk with your kids about money

Talking with kids about money and how to spend it can be difficult for many parents! Don't wait until your kids are teens to help them learn how to save money, how to give it away, and how to spend it wisely. In fact, those three categories are a good way to divide kids' allowances or earnings in a way that reflects your family's faith and the value you place on using God's gifts to serve others.

Talk with your kids about empathy

Ask your kids if they know the meaning of the word; then look it up in the dictionary for a more precise definition. Talk about what it means in terms of real people around you who need help and understanding in a particular situation. Check out world news on the Internet or in your newspaper—and spend some time imagining yourselves into the lives of families torn apart by war, natural disaster, famine, and so forth. Who knows, an act of service or time of prayer may happen as a natural outcome of your conversation!

SESSION **7**

THE CHURCH FAMILY

 **SCRIPTURE**

Deuteronomy 29:9-15; Mark 3:31-35

 FOCUS

Parents need the whole people of God to nurture the faith of their children.

🗨 THINK ABOUT IT (10-15 MINUTES)

How does your church help you nurture your kids' faith? That's the video lead-in question for today's session. If group members weren't able to watch the video prior to your meeting, watch it together as a way of beginning your discussion. Take a few minutes to talk about ways in which your congregation partners with parents to nurture the faith of kids in your church family.

You might also want to set aside a few minutes to talk about how you followed up on the discussion from last time. If you decided to do a service project as a group, update each other on the plan and its progress—or, if you've already completed the project, talk about how it went. How might you follow up for greater impact on the lives and faith of the kids (and adults) who participated?

Or perhaps you chose to have personal conversations with your child(ren) about using money or about the meaning of *empathy*. Share anything from your conversations that might be inspiring or helpful to others in your group. Take a few minutes to encourage and support each other in your efforts to build on the goal of last week's session: helping our children sense the importance of engaging in God's mission in the world.

Here's another possibility for introducing today's discussion that focuses on the important role the whole people of God plays in nurturing children's faith. Check out the quote from the book *Embracing Parents* (see box).

What do you think the authors mean when they say "people should see all kids as their kids"? How easy is this to do? What barriers prevent this from happening? Should it be easier within the context of the church? Why or why not? What are the benefits for the congregation that does see all kids as their kids?

Despite public perception that parents should be solely responsible for raising kids and are doing a poor job of parenting, research clearly shows that those who have strong, supportive connections are more likely to parent better and have better relationships with their children. In addition, when parents are isolated, they are more likely to neglect their kids or abuse them.

Through its research and public leadership, Search Institute has been advocating that people begin to see all kids as their kids, and avoid the my-kids-versus-your-kids mentality. Individuals throughout our society should take a role in raising children and giving parents the support they need. Congregations have an important role to play, as do congregational leaders and members.... Congregations that have taken on this new role have found that not only do young people and parents benefit but so does the congregation and those in it.

—Jolene and Eugene Roehlkepartain, *Embracing Parents:
How Your Congregation Can Strengthen Families*, Abingdon Press 2004, p. 16

🗨 TALK ABOUT IT (30-35 MINUTES)

Spend time reading Scripture and discussing the following questions together. If your time is limited, choose the questions that are most important to your group.

1. Read Deuteronomy 29:9-15 (we suggest you read this passage in *The Message*). What strikes you about God's message to the people of Israel? How do God's words look back over time? How do they look forward to the future? What does being part of God's covenant mean to you today? What does it mean for your children and for the generations to come? If you have time, read the Mark 3:31-35 too. What do you think Jesus meant when he said "Whoever does God's will is my brother and sister and mother"? How

does Jesus' answer connect with the idea that people need to see all kids as their kids?

2. Churches in the Reformed tradition believe that children are full members of Christ's body by virtue of their baptism, but some of us inadvertently contradict this notion by talking about different kinds of membership (baptized members, professing members, full members, and so forth). How does your congregation view its youngest members? Do you think your children feel they are "members in waiting" or "potential members" who just need to grow up and take their rightful places in the church? What can congregations do to emphasize the *full* membership of each child who is a part of the church family?

3. Read the segment of the baptism formulary of the Reformed Church in America (see box on p. 54). Using it as a personal checklist for yourselves, talk about how you're doing at keeping the promises you made at the time your children were baptized. Do the same for the list of promises the congregation made. Why is it so important that *both* parents and congregation take their vows seriously?

At the baptism of infants or young children, the **parents are asked:**
Do you promise
to instruct this child/these children
in the truth of God's Word,
in the way of salvation through Jesus Christ;
to pray for them, to teach them to pray;
and to train them in Christ's way by your example,
through worship, and
in the nurture of the church?
[Parent(s) responds: I do, and I ask God to help me.]

The **congregation responds** to this question:
Do you promise to love, encourage, and support
these brothers and sisters
by teaching the gospel of God's love,
by being an example of Christian faith and character, and
by giving the strong support of God's family
in fellowship, prayer, and service?
[Congregation responds: We do.]

—Reformed Church in America, *Order for the Sacrament of Baptism*, p. 4

4. Do your kids find church to be a warm and welcoming place to go each week? Why or why not? What do your kids appreciate most/least about church? What might you do to make attending church something your children eagerly anticipate? What might your congregation do?

5. John Roberto, editor of the journal *Lifelong Faith*, is passionate about inter-generational faith formation. His approach offers intentional opportunities for the whole congregation to grow in faith together, listening to and learning from each other across the generations. Do you see this happening in your church? How might you introduce the idea—or support and build on

what's already taking place? How have your kids benefited from interacting with older members in your congregation?

Every church can become *intentionally intergenerational!* Most churches are intergenerational or multi-generational by membership. Some churches are *intentionally* intergenerational. They make their intergenerational character a defining feature of their community life, ministries, and programming. These churches make it a priority to foster intergenerational relationships, faith sharing, and storytelling; to incorporate all generations in worship; to develop service projects that involve all ages, and to engage all generations in learning together. For these churches, being intergenerational is a way of life. It is an integral element of their culture. It is who they are!

—John Roberto, "Becoming Intentionally Intergenerational: Models and Strategies," *Lifelong Faith*, volume 3.1, Spring 2009, p. 33

6. Does your church have a separate worship time for young children? Talk about both the benefits and disadvantages of "children's worship." What can parents do to build on young children's understanding of why we worship and how we worship? What can the church do to make congregational worship a time in which children feel welcomed and engaged, not only as participants but also as contributors?

7. Think about the different kinds of families who belong to your church. How can you, as part of the body of Christ, help those with particular needs? Talk about ways your congregation can support, encourage, and nurture the faith of single parents, families going through divorce, families that have a child with a disability, parents who've recently adopted children, families who are living on the edge financially, families whose children have been affected by the death of a family member, and so on.

8. In his book *Helping Our Children Grow in Faith: How the Church Can Nurture the Spiritual Development of Kids*, Robert Keeley reminds us that "faith comes from God. Any fancy curriculum or great words on our part or the part of any teacher or adult can't change the fact that the Holy Spirit has to work in the hearts of people to move them toward God" (p. 11). How does this reminder shape the way you think about your own role—and that of the church—in nurturing and guiding the faith of your children? You may want to pause and pray for the Spirit's presence in your children's lives, in your own lives, and in your church's ministry to children and youth.

9. In what ways has this study and conversation with others helped you in your own faith and in nurturing the faith of your children? How can you build on the relationships you've established and the learning you've done together? Is there a way you can continue to pray for each other, encourage each other, and remain accountable to each other?

◖◗ PRAY ABOUT IT

Take time to pray with (and for!) each other at the end of this session. Be sure to pray in a general way for all the parents and children represented in your group, and encourage everyone to share their needs for continued wisdom and guidance in our God-given responsibilities as faith nurturers of our children.

❗ LIVE IT

Here are a few suggestions for things you might do this week to follow up on the challenges and new insights you've received from each other:

Chat with your kids about church

How many people do your kids know in your church? If your children are young, see how many people they can name and what they remember about them. If your kids are older, ask if there is anyone they especially appreciate or admire or would like to get to know better. Use their answers to help you think more intentionally about building intergenerational relationships in your congregation.

Chat with the pastor or a council/board member

If today's conversation triggered some creativity and enthusiasm for new ways your congregation might strengthen its ministry to children and youth, plan for a way to engage your pastor and/or members of your church governing body in dialogue about faith nurture. Or plan one more session and invite a few decision makers to join you. Tell them what you've talked about over the past seven weeks, and engage them in some energetic brainstorming about ways to work together as parents and congregation to build faith in the kids and teens in your congregation.

Start a prayer group

If your prayer times as a group have been particularly meaningful, keep it going. Share your email addresses so that you can share prayer requests. Commit to praying for each other regularly. (You might want to invite some older members of the congregation to join your group. Grandparents make especially good prayer partners!)

Say thank you

Take a minute to write or email someone from your congregation who has had an influence for good in the life of one of your children. Thank that person for caring about your child and his or her emerging faith!

NOTES